Amazing Biomes

RIVERS AND LAKES

BROWN BEAR BOOKS

Published by Brown Bear Books Ltd

4877 N. Circulo Bujia
Tucson, AZ 85718
USA

and

First Floor
9-17 St. Albans Place
London N1 0NX

ISBN: 978-1-78121-244-8

Library of Congress Cataloging-in-Publication Data
available upon request

Author: Leon Gray
Designer: Karen Perry
Picture Researcher: Clare Newman
Editor: Tim Harris
Children's Publisher: Anne O'Daly
Design Manager: Keith Davis
Editorial Director: Lindsey Lowe

Manufactured in the United States of America

CPSIA compliance information: Batch# AG/5567

Picture Credits

The photographs in this book are used by permission
and through the courtesy of:

T=Top, C=Center, B=Bottom, L=Left, R=Right

Front cover: main, ©Mike Lane/FLPA;
background, ©Shutterstock.
Interior: 1, ©Nattanan726/Shutterstock;
2-3, ©Dmitry Naumov/Shutterstock; 4-5, ©RIRF Stock/
Shutterstock; 5cr, ©Tony Campbell/Shutterstock;
6cl, ©Bebay/Shutterstock; 6bl, ©Anton Ivanoc/
Shutterstock; 6bc, ©Matthew Dixon/Shutterstock;
7tr, ©Mikhail Markovsky/Shutterstock; 7cr, ©Fritz 16/
Shutterstock; 7bl, ©Przemyslaw Skibiriski/Shutterstock;
8-9, ©Frank11/Shutterstock; 9cr, ©Tomaz Kunst/
Shutterstock; 10, ©Alice Nerr/Shutterstock; 11c, ©Max
Mindenthaler/Shutterstock; 11br, ©Mickolay Vinokirov/
Shutterstock; 12, ©Luck Luckyfarm/Shutterstock;
13, ©rdonar/Shutterstock; 14, ©Wildnedpix/
Shutterstock; 15, ©Wikipedia; 16, ©HTU/Shutterstock;
17, ©John Carnemo Ila/Dreamstime; 18bl, ©Kim Taylor/
Nature PL/Corbis; 19tr, ©Hamsterman/Shutterstock;
19, ©Ongm/Dreamstime; 20, ©Andre Anita/
Shutterstock; 21tr, ©Petr Podrouzek/Shutterstock;
21br, ©Ignacia Sulavena/Shutterstock;
22-23, ©Nattanan726/Shutterstock; 23cr, ©De Visu/
Shutterstock; 24, ©Pete Spiro/Shutterstock; 24t, ©Ivan
Sazykin/Shutterstock; 25br, ©Aneese/iStock/Thinkstock;
26-27, ©gopixgo/Shutterstock; 27tr, ©Christian
Draghici/Shutterstock; 28cl, ©Mickolay Vinokirov/
Shutterstock; 28cr, ©Mickolay Vinokirov/Shutterstock;
28b ©Ongm/Dreamstime; 29c, ©Luck Luckyfarm/
Shutterstock; 29b, ©De Visu/Shutterstock.

Brown Bear Books has made every attempt to contact
the copyright holder. If you have any information
please contact licensing@brownbearbooks.co.uk

All other photographs and artworks © Brown Bear Books Ltd.

Contents

• • • • • • • • • • • • →

INTRODUCTION

Water is one of the reasons that life on Earth is possible. Rivers and lakes are important **sources** of water. These freshwater biomes are home to many different animals and plants. We also rely on rivers for fresh drinking water and water to help crops grow.

A bald eagle plucks a salmon from Chilkat Lake, Alaska.

Biomes are places where plants or animals live and grow. Some animals and plants live in grasslands or dry deserts. Some live in, on, or beside rivers and lakes. Rivers are channels of fresh water that wind across the land. Most begin high up in hills and mountains and flow down to the sea. Lakes and ponds are pools of water that fill hollow **basins** in the land. Some stretches of water, such as giant inland seas, contain salty water.

Read on to find out what rivers and lakes are like—and how plants, animals, and people live in, on, and around them.

HIGH POINT

Snake River, Idaho, starts life as tiny mountain streams. As water flows down the slopes, the streams join to form the giant winding river.

5

WORLD RIVERS AND

Rivers and lakes are found all over the world. This map shows some of the major rivers and lakes to be found on the world's continents.

The city of Chicago, Illinois, is built on the shores of Lake Michigan.

NORTH
AMERICA

SOUTH
AMERICA

The Amazon River flows through the Amazon rain forest in South America. It is 4,000 miles (6,400 kilometers) long.

The city of Lond
in England is bu
along the banks
the River Thames

ANTARCTI

LAKES

RIVERS AND
LAKES

EUROPE

ASIA

Lake Baikal in Russia contains 20 percent of the world's supply of fresh water.

A paddle steamer cruises along the Murray River in southern Australia.

ICA

AUSTRALIA

A rainbow forms as water from the Zambezi River, on the border between Zambia and Zimbabwe in Africa, spills over Victoria Falls.

CLIMATE

Rivers and lakes play a vital role in the **water cycle**, which helps shape the weather on our planet. They also have some of the most varied climates of all Earth's biomes.

LIFELINE

The Nile in Egypt, on the African continent, is the world's longest river. It carries water through the Sahara Desert, allowing crops to be grown along its banks.

Water is constantly recycled around our planet. It moves between air, land, and the oceans. This movement is called the water cycle. Sunlight warms the water in rivers, lakes, and oceans. This water **evaporates** and rises to form clouds. The clouds get bigger and heavier until they eventually release water as rain or snow. Most of it ends up back in the rivers and oceans.

Heavy rain clouds over Lake Victoria in Uganda, Africa.

Changing Climate

Rivers and lakes are very different from place to place. In polar regions, the water in rivers and lakes freezes over for most of the year. In deserts, it can be so hot that the water evaporates. Rivers and lakes dry up and disappear. Some rivers regularly flood the surrounding land. This can destroy biomes and the homes of people who live there. Rivers also shape the land. The flowing water grinds away the rock, carving **valleys** in the landscape. The river carries the **sediment** to the sea, where it is released.

Tepuis mountain

BIO FACT

Angel Falls in Venezuela, South America, is the world's tallest waterfall at 3,212 feet (979 meters). Clouds form above the forests on the tepuis (tabletop) mountain. The rain then feeds the waterfall.

WOW!

- Lake Eyre in Australia lies in a desert and is usually almost dry. If heavy rain falls in mountains far to the north, rivers carry water into the lake. When it is full, the lake is 20 feet (6 meters) deep.

It is easier to travel by snowmobile when the Mackenzie River freezes over during the Canadian winter.

Dead Sea

The Dead Sea is a salt lake on the border of Israel and Jordan in the Middle East. Water flows into the Dead Sea from rivers and streams, but no water flows out. This water dissolves rocks at the bottom of the lake. The sun then evaporates the water, making the lake very salty. In fact, it is so salty that no animals and plants can live there.

PLANTS

Many different plants depend on rivers and lakes for their survival. Some live in the water, while others cling to rocks or grow on the riverbanks.

The most common plants found in rivers and lakes are so small that you need a **microscope** to see them. They are called **algae**, and they are not true plants. These tiny **organisms** do not have roots, stems, and leaves. Algae make food in the same way as plants, using energy from the sun. Algae are eaten by many of the animals that live in rivers and lakes.

Water Lilies

Plants called water lilies live in the deeper parts of some ponds and lakes. Their waxy leaves and colorful flowers float on the surface of the water. The stems grow up from the bed of the lake or pond toward the sunlight.

ON THE ROCKS

Simple plants called mosses and liverworts grow on rocks in rivers. The roots cling tightly onto the surface of the rocks, so the plants are not swept away by the water current.

BIO FACT

Lake Natron in Tanzania, Africa, is too salty to support plant growth. Instead, tiny salt-loving organisms live in the water. They give the lake its deep red color.

Amazon Floods

During the rainy season, the Amazon River bursts its banks. Water floods the surrounding forest to form lagoons. This flooding is an important process. The water returns important **nutrients** to the soil. When the floodwater levels subside, new plants take root and renew the rain forest.

Water Weeds

Many plants thrive in the nutrient-rich waters of rivers and lakes. In fact, some plants, such as duckweed and water hyacinth, grow so well that people view them as **weeds**. These plants grow very quickly, and the leaves spread out to cover the surface of the water. They crowd out other plants that grow in the water. Eventually, the dense carpet of vegetation stops oxygen from reaching the water below, which can suffocate the animals that live underwater.

Water crowfoot is a common water weed found in the rivers of North America and Europe.

ANIMALS

Numerous types of animals live in or near rivers and lakes. Some spend all of their lives in water. Others grow up in water but leave when they become adults. Many simply visit to feed or drink.

GONE FISHING

A kingfisher plucks a fish from the surface of a lake. These birds have sharp, pointy beaks to spear their slippery **prey**.

More than one-third of the world's 25,000 fish **species** live in freshwater rivers and lakes. Many insect **larvae** (young) develop in water and leave when they become adults. **Amphibians**, such as frogs, follow a similar life cycle.

Many other animals use rivers and lakes as hunting grounds. Birds such as bald eagles and ospreys swoop down to catch fish from the water's surface. **Mammals**, such as otters and voles, hunt in rivers and live in burrows in the riverbanks.

Rudderlike tail

Shape of bill is same as a duck's bill

Webbed feet

Sharp claws

Duckbill Platypus

The duckbill platypus lives in rivers and creeks in Australia. This unusual mammal is well adapted to life in the water. It has sleek, waterproof fur, a broad tail, and webbed feet, which help it to swim quickly. Unlike most other mammals, the platypus lays eggs instead of giving birth to live young. She raises them in a tunnel in the riverbank.

Fishy Food Chain

Fish are perfectly adapted to life in rivers and lakes. With their streamlined shape, scaly bodies, and powerful fins, many different fish thrive in these freshwater biomes. These animals are an important link in the **food chains** of rivers and lakes. Fish eat a wide range of food. Some feed on microscopic algae, trapping the tiny organisms on their **gills**. Most eat other animals, such as insects and other fish. The fish themselves provide food for many other animals, such as otters and seals.

Waterproof fur

SEAL LIFE
Baikal seals (right) live in the landlocked waters of Lake Baikal in Siberia, Russia. They are the only seals to spend all their lives in fresh water.

A young brown trout leaps from the surface of the water to catch a passing damselfly.

Feeding Frenzy

The red-bellied piranha is one of the most fearsome **predators** of the Amazon. These meat-eating fish swim in shoals in the rivers that flow through the rain forest. The piranhas are mainly **scavengers** but sometimes go into a "feeding frenzy," using their sharp teeth to rip apart prey, such as other fish.

Nostrils close when underwater

Third eyelid covers each eye

Sharp claws

Water Predators

Strong swimmers, such as otters, and reptiles, such as alligators and crocodiles, are deadly predators in rivers and lakes. The grizzly bear is another predator that hunts in some rivers in North America. Every year, wild salmon return from the oceans to lay their eggs in rivers. The bears pluck the salmon from the water as the fish swim upstream against the current.

A grizzly bear catches a salmon. The bears feast on salmon returning to rivers to lay their eggs.

RIVER KILLER

Dragonflies are deadly predators. The young **nymphs** live in water and snatch passing prey. The winged adults snatch other flying insects in midair.

Crocodile Attack

Crocodiles are predators that hunt in warm, tropical river and lake biomes. These **reptiles** are **carnivores** and will eat anything they can catch, from fish to small mammals. Large crocodiles regularly attack people. They are very quick and strike before their prey can react.

21

PEOPLE

People have always relied on rivers and lakes for survival. We use the fresh water to drink and to clean our bodies and our clothes. Today, many people enjoy river sports such as canoeing and rafting.

In developing countries, people still fish rivers and lakes for food and hunt the animals that live near them. In fact, many modern cities have developed from the small villages people built along rivers and lakes. Some rivers and lakes are so important that many people consider them to be sacred places. The Ganges River in India is sacred (holy) to many people.

Farmers also rely on rivers and lakes. A river's natural cycle of flooding adds nutrients to the soil, making it easier for farmers to grow crops. Rivers and lakes also provide water for the crops. This is called **irrigation**.

FISH SUPPER

A fisherman rows out to catch fish from Lake Inle in Burma. Fish is the main food for people living beside the lake.

Hindus bathe in the Ganges River. The river is sacred to them.

On the Move

Before the age of motor transportation, people often relied on rivers to move around. They could transport themselves and their goods much more easily than walking across the land. The first boats were made by tying logs together with strong reeds. Later, people hollowed out logs to make canoes and propelled them through the water using oars. Eventually, people harnessed the power of the wind and built huge sailing ships. Explorers sailed across the oceans in these ships to discover new lands.

CANAL FACTS

In many parts of the world, people have built canals to transport people and their belongings. The Panama Canal is the world's longest canal. It links the Pacific and Atlantic oceans in Central America.

Yachts crowd a marina on Lake Michigan at the Chicago waterfront. Sailing is a popular hobby for many people.

Thrill-seekers take part in a whitewater rafting race on the Belaya River in Russia.

River Cruise

A paddle steamer takes tourists on a cruise down the Mississippi River in the United States. These boats were once used to transport people and goods along rivers. The steam engines have been replaced with modern diesel engines.

THE FUTURE

Rivers and lakes are some of our most varied and beautiful biomes, but their future remains uncertain. Human activities are damaging them and the plants and animals that live in them.

One of the major causes for concern is **pollution**. Human activities, such as farming and industry, pollute rivers and lakes. The harmful chemicals from factories and farms run off the land and end up in rivers and lakes. As they build up in the water, the chemicals kill the animals and plants that live there.

Climate change is another problem for rivers and lakes. As Earth's temperature increases, the water in rivers and lakes dries up. Many countries are also building dams across rivers to generate electricity from the water. This disrupts the river's natural flow, which then harms the animals and plants that live farther upstream.

Dead fish are a telltale sign of river pollution. Toxic chemicals build up in the bodies of the fish and kill them.

ARAL SEA

The Aral Sea was once a huge lake in central Asia. Rivers that flowed into it were blocked, so the lake has shrunk to a fraction of its former size.

QUIZ

Try this quiz to test your knowledge of rivers and lakes. You can find the answers on page 31.

1 Which European capital city is built along the banks of the River Thames?

2 The Dead Sea gets its name because no animals or plants can live there. Why?

3 These seals live in a landlocked lake in the middle of Siberia in Russia. What is the name of this lake?

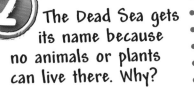

28

4 What plant lives on the surface of some ponds and lakes and has these colorful flowers?

Fact File

○ Most rivers start as small streams high in the mountains and flow down to the sea.

○ Lakes form when water collects in basins in the land.

○ Rivers are an important source of fresh water for animals, plants, and people.

○ Water moves between the air, land, and sea in a journey called the water cycle.

○ Human activities such as farming and dam-building are destroying rivers and lakes.

5 The Ganges River in India is sacred to people from which religion?

Winners and Losers

⬆ Otters have become more common in Britain's rivers. That is because many chemicals that harmed the otters in the past have now been banned.

⬇ There are now no river dolphins living in the Yangtze River in China. They died out because they got caught up in fishing nets or collided with boats.

GLOSSARY

algae: Tiny plantlike organisms that live in rivers and lakes.

amphibians: Animals, such as frogs, that start life in the water but move onto the land as adults.

basin: A hollow in the surface of the land into which water drains to form a lake.

carnivores: Animals that eat only meat. Crocodiles are carnivores.

evaporate: To change from a liquid to a gas. Water from rivers and lakes evaporates to form clouds.

freshwater: Refers to water that is fresh, such as rivers, lakes, and streams, and not of the sea.

food chain: The order in which animals feed on plants and other animals within a biome.

gills: The breathing organs of fish and other animals. The gills absorb oxygen, allowing animals to breathe underwater.

irrigation: The use of water from rivers and lakes to water crops.

larvae: The young form of animals such as insects and amphibians.

mammals: Animals with warm blood that breathe air using lungs. Mammals feed their young on milk.

microscope: An instrument that people use to see extremely small objects, such as algae.

nutrients: Substances that provide food for growth.

nymphs: The young of some kinds of insects before they change to their adult form.

organisms: A scientific word to describe any living thing, such as an animal or plant.

pollution: Human-made chemicals that harm the environment.

predators: Animals that hunt and eat other animals.

prey: Animals that are hunted and eaten by other animals.

reptiles: Animals that usually have scaly skin and lay eggs. Crocodiles, snakes, and turtles are reptiles.

scavengers: Animals that feed on the remains of dead animals.

sediment: Fine material, such as mud and sand, carried by rivers.

sources: Places where something comes from.

species: A group of animals that look alike. Members of the same species can mate and produce young together.

valleys: A deep groove cut into the land by the force of flowing water.

water cycle: The journey that water takes as its moves between the air, land, and the oceans.

weeds: Plants that crowd out cultivated plants.

FURTHER RESOURCES

Books

Beatty, Richard. *Rivers, Lakes, Streams, and Ponds* (Biomes Atlases). North Mankato, MN: Raintree, 2010.

Johnson, Jinny. *River and Lake Life* (Watery Worlds). Collingwood, ON: Smart Apple Media, 2011.

Kaye, Carole Berger. *Make a Splash!: A Kid's Guide to Protecting Our Oceans, Lakes, Rivers, & Wetlands.* Minneapolis, MN: Free Spirit Publishing, 2012.

Parker, Steve. *Pond and River* (DK Eyewitness Books). New York: Dorling Kindersley, 2011.

Websites

Kids Do Ecology: Freshwater
kids.nceas.ucsb.edu/biomes/
freshwater.html
Find out about the animals, plants, and terrain of freshwater biomes at this informative site. Including information about aquatic ecosystems around lakes, rivers, and wetlands.

Kidskonnect: Lake Facts
kidskonnect.com/geography/lakes/
Learn amazing facts about lake biomes including the Great Lakes, the largest body of fresh water on Earth. With links to related topics.

National Geographic: Freshwater
environment.national geographic.
com/environment/photos/
freshwater-plants-animals/
View spectacular photos of the world's freshwater biomes, and read about the plants and animals that inhabit them.

World Wildlife Fund: Freshwaters
www.worldwildlife.org/habitats/
freshwaters
Check out cool footage of river and lake animals, such as river dolphins and otters, and read about freshwater biome conservation plans.

Answers to the quiz: **1** London. **2** Because the water is too salty. **3** Lake Baikal. **4** Water lily. **5** Hindu.

INDEX